TABLE OF CONTENT

INTRODUCTION

This is a perfect guide to make your own household disinfectant, sprays or wipes to destroy the virus and other bacteria causing issues, which is a worry shared by everyone right now.

The CDC recommends many ways to defend you and your household against the virus by the end of March 2020. One is distancing oneself from society. One is about frequent washing of hands with soap.

The third is the regular disinfection of surfaces and items. In the words of the CDC: 'This consists of tables, doorknobs, light switches, countertops, handles, desks, telephones, keyboards, toilets, rocket and sinks.'

The virus is known to survive on plastics and steel over three days, but the number of live viruses declines quickly over that time. The products discussed in this book are safe to use on all of these surfaces, but manufacturer guidelines should always be followed, since bleach-like disinfectants can affect other surfaces and soft materials.

Many people are concerned that packages and mails can carry the virus to their homes. The virus will live on carton boxes for up to 24 hours, but the opinion of the CDC is that "due to the poor survival of such viruses on the surface, there is probably very low risk of spreading from products or packaging shipped at ambient temperatures for a time period of days or weeks."

The fact that we have taken care of your interaction with these surfaces is just as important — and perhaps more important — the way you treat the products.

A spray, disinfectant or wipe can destroy almost any form of bacteria and virus to be considered disinfectant, and must destroy almost 100% of the pathogens present on the surface on which it is used.

The disinfectants vary from sanitizers that "are not meant to kill all microorganisms that cause disease," "They are designed to kill most, to a level considered safe," and "get into play on non-disinfected surfaces — porous surfaces such as your skin, fabric, and carpet."

Antimicrobial and antibacterial are other words that you might have seen in home cleaners and soap. "This is not sanitizing or disinfecting,". "The household cleaners and hand soaps are said. It is really a bit marketing.

"The FDA has studied antimicrobial soaps and their active ingredients extensively and has determined that" manufacturers have shown that these ingredients are no more effective than plain soap and water in preventing disease and the spread of certain infections.

Disinfectants and sprayers are usually designed to be employed on hard, non-porous surfaces such as metal (faucets, doorbells), countertops (quartz, granite sealed), or glass and ceramic surfaces (sinks, tiles, pipes).

These do not work on soft or absorbent materials, such as fabrics or rugs, so they may cause irreparable harm in the case of bleach disinfectants.

Let's get started

CHAPTER 1: Homemade Multi-Purpose Disinfectant And Spray

Right now is the best time for a mild disinfectant spray to be put into regular use or should I say a replacement for the stuff found on the shelves? I am confident that most of us have vivid memories of heavily fragrant sprays because of their common use in restaurants, homes and even schools.

Disinfecting is a (usually) after-cleaning task which, in my view, should be done much less frequently at home. "Disinfecting ... this means killing or rendering a high percentage of the germs unable to reproduce."

Disinfecting is more than just soil, fat or dust. I think it is not necessary to periodically clean all surfaces in a contemporary home due to indoor plumbing and good hygiene.

Through flu, cold, and virus seasons, homemade sanitizing items will make the difference between staying healthy and getting sick, keeping the hands and surfaces clean. Thorough washing your hands with water and soap will still be your first protection against germs, but these DIY items can also aid in a pinch. These basic items for DIY sanitization will enable you to clean your hands and other surfaces to destroy germs.

Sanitizing Hand Spray

Hand Spray is primarily made of isopropyl alcohol, the most effective component for germ killing. Under the absence of isopropyl alcohol, vodka or ever clear may also be used.

The essential oil mix here is known as theft oil, known for its disinfecting properties. It also helps the spray smell nice while aloe and vitamin E add conditioning to keep any of the alcohol in the spray from drying your hands.

2 tablespoons 70% or higher ingredients isopropyl alcohol or 1 ever clear vitamin E capsule 10 drops the remaining 2 tablespoon of aloe Vera distilled water

Directions

Fill in the 3 ounce spray bottle of alcohol or vodka.

Using a pin to pinch the vitamin E capsule and press into the flask 6 drops of vitamin E juice.

Add oil and aloe Vera.

Top with water.

Shake vigorously and use as a side spray.

If you have no oil, you may use 10 drops of all essential disinfectant oils, including lavender, thyme, eucalyptus, cinnamon, peppermint, clove orange or oregano oils. You can also make your own thefts and add them to sanitary devices or disseminate them in your room.

Combine the same quantity of the following essential oil in an amber-colored bottle: Clove Eucalyptus Cinnamon Bark Lemon Rosemary to improve anti-germ properties, add oil to a disinfectant recipe.

Apply 2 to 3 drops to 1 tablespoon of carrier oil, such as cocoon oil, if the oil is to be used directly. Never place undiluted essential oil on the skin directly.

CHAPTER 2: DIY Antibacterial Cleaning Wipes

The toughest thing to find is a sticky glass jar that is big enough to accommodate a roll of paper towels.

However, the paper towels may also be removed and placed into a jar to achieve the same results.

Ingredients

1 sheet of paper towels 1 cup of ever clear or 70 percent or more isopropyl alcohol 1 tablespoon soap with 10 drops with oil from a burglary, or another essential oil disinfectant. 2 cup of warm water diluted.

Combine the alcohol or whiskey, dish soap, theft oil and distilled water in a large glass picture or cup. Mix well. Mix well.

Pour over the towels of paper. Keep and let the towels absorb the fluid for about 30 minutes.

In one direction, clean the surfaces.

Cleaning Tissue Paper DIY Antibacterial hand soap

The most effective way to destroy germs on your hands is to daily use soap and water and wash your hands properly. However, you can make antibacterial hand soap if you find you need any extra disinfectant during the cold and flu season.

Combining the castille broth, the oregano oil, the Tea Tree Oil and the orange oil.

Ingredients
4 ounces liquid castile soap
10 drops oregano oil
10 drop orange essential oil.

Instructions
Shake to blend
You can swap just 30 drops of theft oil for the essential oils.

Tips to reduce germs
There are several additional tips for sanitizing your health that are useful for protecting your hands and sanitizing your surfaces.

To prevent contaminating surfaces, use sterile towels or paper towels while washing surfaces and drying hands.

Wash your hands frequently, especially after you have been out of home or in a sick person's room. Scrub your hands with soap at least 20 seconds before rinsing, to remove the sprouts.

Sprinkle dirty surfaces thoroughly and let the cleaners sit on them for four minutes until they are cleaned with a clean towel or a rag.

Do not reuse sanitizing towels.

Do not use sponges that are hard to sanitize and can retain bacteria.

Take hand sanitizer while you are out public, but use it pinch; it is not a substitute for thorough hand washing, which is your first line of germ protection.

If someone in your house is sick, place the person in quarantine in a bedroom and bathroom and disinfect all surfaces in the house. Additionally: Using disposable silverware and cups to serve food on plate. Discharge in a dust bag reserved only for such dishes kept outside the building.

Wash hands after visiting the sick rooms thoroughly.

Wash laundry and put it into a laundry pan so that you do not "hug" the bedding that may be tainted.

Sanitize all surfaces, including remote controls, light switches, thieves, mobile phones, computer keyboards or whatever else the person touches, until the person is again safe.

Limit your exposure to germs

While germs do not need to be phobic, they allow you to be vigilant even in the course of outbreaks of cold, flu or other diseases. Limit your exposure to germs by washing and/or sanitizing your hands regularly and avoiding any places where bacteria or viruses can be found. You will reduce the risk of being sick by taking care of hygiene activities.

CHAPTER 3: How To Make DIY All-Purpose Disinfectant Cleaners

There are plenty of viruses out there. In peak times it can be difficult to try to find cleaning products, such as Lysol wipes and multifunctional cleaners. Fortunately, you do have disinfectants in your pantry.

To make all-intentional DIY cleansers for the elimination of germs, learn how to use essential oils, hydrogen peroxide, white vinegar and even alcohol. What would you do to automatically disinfect?

When it comes to naturally disinfecting your home, there are a couple of primary cleaners out there.

These can be used alone or together to get rid of the bad viruses and bacteria which cause SARS, H1N1, staph and more. The best non-toxic natural disinfectants are:

- 3 percent hydrogen peroxide
- White vinegar
- Homemade Dry Erase Board Cleaner,
- Strongly proven vodka (same cheap vodka)

These are the best natural disinfectants which can kill bacteria and germs which can make you sick. They are also safe to use with pets and babies. Since you understand the basics, check out a couple of all-round DIY disinfectant cleaners you can make in your console with materials.

As these are the best natural disinfectants, most DIY cleaners will use these different materials. Other materials you will need. You will need:

- 70 percent iso-propyl alcohol / rubbing alcohol (vodka substitute)
- Dawn antibacterial
- Glass spray bottle (glass preferably)
- Essential oils (thyme, tea tree, cinnamon have some of the highest antiviral characteristics)
- If you have no vodka on your hand, you can substitute rubbing alcohol.

Instructions

Fill about 1/3 of it with vodka in a glass or plastic spray bottle.

Complete another 1/3 of hot water.

Remove 30-50 drops of, thyme, essential oil tea tree or cinnamon.

Fill with vinegar the remaining third.

Shake well.

Sprinkle any surfaces you need to scrub.

Just let it dry for a couple of minutes.

Using a cleaning cloth

You would like to use this carefully for granite or marble surfaces, but for general viral and antibacterial cleaning it is free. You may also opt to add rubbing alcohol, but be careful not to use it because it may be unpleasant when breathed or eaten.

If you are searching for something safe to use on your granite counters, you are going to work with alcohol and castle soap. You will: take a spray bottle to this DIY disinfectant, preferably glass but plastic fits in the pinch.

In a bottle add 1/2 cup of vodka and 1-1/2 cups of hot water. It does not have to be precise, just using the bottle. You are looking for approximately 1 piece of vodka to 3 pieces of tea.

Add Castile soap in a tea cubicle and 20 drops of hot tea tree oil. (If you do not like the odor of tea tree oil, you should apply some lavender to combat the odor.)

Spray your surfaces down and allow them to sit down for a couple of minutes to get rid of all those nasty germs.

Such recipes should work without them if you have no essential oils. The primary force combatant is alcohol.

Homemade All-Purpose Cleaner

Add a small amount of disinfectant help and provide an effective cleaner to kill viruses instantly. This formula can be used with alcohol or vinegar rubbing, depending on what you have.

Instruction

Take a spray bottle to make your life simpler.

Mix 2 to 3 cups of hot water in 1/2 cup of rubber alcohol or vinegar.

Remove 2-3 Dawn antibacterial soap squirts.

Give it a bit of a shake.

Start disinfecting from your counters to the surfaces of the bathroom.

The acidity of vinegar will deteriorate the sealant in Marble and granite; therefore, if you want to use vinegar, you should not use this recipe on these surfaces.

For essential oils, natural oils are a perfect way to clean if you have got them. Not only can you spread them in the air, there are also cleaning recipes that use essential oils.

You will need to follow these steps for this recipe.

Place 1/4 to 1/2 cup of vinegar in a spray bottle.

Apply 20 or so drops of essential cinnamon oil or thyme. You may also use a pinch of tea tree.

Fill with hot water.

Give it a shake to sprinkle and blend.

Allow the mixture to sit for 1-2 minutes on the surfaces.

Use the rag to wipe any surfaces down.

With essential oils, it is better to use a glass spray bottle because the oils will break the plastic down.

CHAPTER 4: Homemade Disinfectant Spray and Hand Sanitizer

For a global virus pandemic now in progress, personal protection against the spread of the virus should be assured. We must protect ourselves and prevent anyone from being polluted.

Knowing the difference between cleaning and disinfecting a surface is important. Cleaning destroys germs and reduces the risk of infection. After a surface has been washed, disinfecting destroys germs by chemical means. To prevent the spread of disease, it is important to complete both steps.

The CDC(suggest three basic disinfectants.

- Hydrogen peroxide
- Alcohol
- Bleach

Everyone has different personal protection and sanitation guidelines.

Hydrogen peroxide

A 3 percent hydrogen peroxide concentration can be used alone or decontaminated to 0.5 percent.

Disinfectant Spray
1/4 cup 3% hydrogen peroxide
1 cup of water spray bottle
Instruction
Mix the ingredients in a sprayer.
Spritz your hands or surfaces and allow the solution to sit for a minute at least

before wiping.

2/3 cup isopropyl alcool (70% -99%)

1/3 cup aloe vera gel

Well screened dispenser

Blend alcohol and aloe Vera gel to make your hand sanitizer.

In at least 30 seconds, the hand sanitizer must be "sitting on your skin" to fully disinfect. A mixture that contains at least 60% alcohol effectively destroys virus pathogens according to CDC (1).

Alcohol

CDC (2) advises that 70% isopropyl alcohol or 60% ethanol should be used.
The FDA(3) advises the use of isopropyl alcohol in hand sanitizers of at least 75%.
The University of Rutgers (4) recommends at least 70% alcohol.
Alcohol and water can also be used to cleanse hard surfaces, but they can be rough on the skin and not approved for this reason.
Be sure that every alcoholic disinfectant is stored in a well-secured bottle to prevent it from evaporating.

Bleach

Based 1/3 of blue bleach
1 gallon of cold water
Wear gloves for use with countertops, doorknobs, remote tables, etc.
Using the liquid within 24 hours, as the disinfectant weakens.
At least 30 seconds of decontamination, but ten minutes of treatment is optimal. Bleach house is suitable for the sterilization of most surfaces.
Be mindful that most items are damaged or lost if they are exposed to bleach.
Do not use bleach to sanitize your hands as it can damage your skin!
Never mix with bleach ammonia or other cleaning substance!

CHAPTER 5: How To Make A Non-Bleach Disinfectant Spray

This spray is a non-bleach disinfectant, so it is safe on textiles, but only on hard surfaces to eliminate virus.

Lysol aerosols use quaternary (quats) ammonium to kill viruses and have an EPA list N to stay for 10 minutes, the time it takes for it to sit on a surface to eliminate the virus.

The Lysol Kitchen Pro spray is quats-based but only has two minutes to sit.

Sprays can be used safely on almost any solid surface and will not harm most materials, but will not guarantee the disinfection of soft surfaces. (These surfaces can be 'sanitized,' meaning removal of a high percentage of bacteria, but not all of them.)

Three bleach-based sprays, including metals (such as rods) and pottery (tiles, quartz, porcelain), are only suitable for the use of hard surfaces because bleach affects many of the materials. Bleach also creates toxic fumes and is harsh on the skin. Be sure to breathe and wear gloves if you use either of these bleach-based sprays.

Many more commonly distributed sprays, aerosols and liquids are classified N in the EPA, which means that they are licensed for proper use to destroy the latest virus. If you have any of them or can find them, they are trustworthy.

Two more popular are:

Clorox Solutions Advanced Formula Disinfecting Remover and

Clorox Scentiva Bathroom Disinfecting Cleaner (hydrogen peroxides, five minutes spent dwelling time, bottle of spray or liquid).

For disinfection purposes, we do not suggest toilet-bowl cleaners because they are thickened gels that stick to the toilet surfaces and are thus hard to wash off – a crucial move towards proper disinfection.

The other "RTU's" in List N are intended for medical, medicinal and professional cleaning services. During the past, some were sold through Amazon and other general retailers, but we did not find any in stock. When you want to perform your own search, List N scanning for "RTU" will take all of these things one by one.

Take note of the column for "Active Ingredient / s," because others are made from bleach (sodium hypochlorite) that can damage other surfaces. Others based on quaternary ammonium (quats) are normally fabric secure but ensure that viruses are removed on hard surfaces only.

The same applies to hydrogen peroxide-based men. In all situations, take the right precautions, including wearing kitchen gloves and maintaining adequate ventilation.

Diluted in water, bleach is the main component of a home-made disinfectant, which is as powerful as harmful. Figure out how to treat bleach safely and deal with it if you are new to it.

A combination of regular household bleach and water will disinfect virus hard surfaces. If you have bleach, you can make your own blend and sprinkle it with a spray bottle or towels.

For use with standard bleach, different sources offer different bleach-to-water ratios.

The CDC claims "[u]nexpired bleach will work against viruses" in 1:48 (1⁄3 cup of leaven per gallon of water or 4 teaspoons per quarter).

Slightly stronger 1:32 (1⁄2 cup per gallon or 2 teaspoons per quarter), Clorox recommends. I suggest a slightly higher 1:10 ratio (approximately 11⁄2 cups per gallon or about 1⁄3 cup / quarter). Some medical disinfectants are exactly the same solution (for example Clorox Healthcare Bleach Germicidal Cleaner).

Whatever ratio you use, try to invest the 10-minute dwelling time: Warner told us that this is a new or unknown pathogen guideline in the EPO, and it is also a time of residence for daily householder bleaches in the EPO's N List.

When removed from its original storage container, Bleach degrades relatively easily and is less successful every day. Save the container away from light will prolong the useful life of the container. When your bottle of bleach is full, add a little more to the mix and try to find a fresh bottle if possible.

These mixtures can be used only on hard surfaces — they permanently ruin the majority of fabrics and many other soft materials — and they are difficult to work with.

Wear shoes and socks and as much as possible, ventilate the room. "Bleach, if the vapors are corrosive," "If it give you a sore throat, do not taste dinner, and, the next day, you might wake up with a strange taste in the mouth."

It must also be cleaned off after 10 minutes of living as bleach can be left to sit indefinitely and destroy durable materials such as steel. And some plastic containers will break down over time.

Once you start mixing bleach solutions, particularly if you are fresh, make sure to read thoroughly the entire warning label on the bleach bottle and take caution in store, handling and cleaning afterwards. Data on avoiding "irreversible damage to the eye and skin" is worth your time.

So never mix blueberry with any ammonia or ammonia (like many vent cleaners) or something acidic (like white vinegar and other lime or rust removers such as CLR or Bar Keepers Friend). Each can contain highly dangerous and even lethal gases.

CHAPTER 6: How To Clean And Disinfect Yourself, Your Home, And Your Stuffs

These are our in-depth best practices to keep you safe and virus free (and almost everything else).

You have heard it a million times already, and you can hear it a million more, but the best way for you to decrease the chance of contracting virus (or passing it on to someone else) is to wash the hand anytime you cough, sneeze, touch your nose, use the bathroom or leave one location for another. Before you leave and return from the grocery store, for instance, you can wash your hands.

If you find some, hand sanitizer is a quick and wonderful cleaning tool. Hand sanitizer does not, however, substitute washing your hands with soap and water. Soap and water will also make the hands a little smoother. You do not automatically destroy all bacteria, but it will wash them off when you wash your hands correctly.

The World Health Organization has detailed guidelines on how to do the hand washing correctly for 20 seconds (which we all have seen in meme form). It is also necessary to moisturize your hands freely.

Dry, broken skin is more at risk of all kinds of infection, so add a little moisturizer after washing. It is nice!

Most hydrating lotions have identical ingredients, beginning with water and glycerin, so the brand really does not matter.

Even if you are not sick, stay home if you can. It is an unnecessary risk not only for yourself, but for people around you to be in big crowds or go to restaurants.

The more visible you are, the more chances the latest virus will have to take your face, clothes or person for a trip. The virus is very vulnerable to millions of people. This also puts them at risk if you put yourself at risk.

"There will be a large proportion of people who have aged or other illnesses and if they all get sick at once, they will overwhelm the health care system." Dr. John Townes, Chief of Infection Prevention and

Does the clothes washing machine work?

Yeah, most of the time

Just wash your garments at a slightly higher temperature with daily laundry soap and dry it than you might otherwise do is do whatever you can to disinfect your clothes.

Be sure that everything, including the hamper and your hands, are disinfected, particularly if you have a sick person in the house.

Clean and disinfect the barrier like any surface and, after treating dirty laundry of someone who is sick, wash thoroughly. The CDC suggests the use of a liner.

You should not forget your coat and jacket washing.

Do you have to disinfect foods?

According to the FDA no evidence indicates that food or food packaging cannot spread the newer virus, and food or food packaging need not currently be disinfected more than you would normally. Just follow normal food protection and wash your hands.

How to disinfect your machines

This is where it can be difficult to clean and disinfect. Your devices that all keep you safe during self-isolation but, as we all know, they are germ magnets. They are high-touch surfaces that you take around with you, so that you have to clean and disinfect them.

To stop repeating myself, just say this here: the safest way to clean your machines is to disinfect wipes, hands down.

Nevertheless, other apps have different requirements.

How to clean your phone or tablet

If you have a disinfecting wipes or alcohol solution (at least 70%) on an iPhone or Android phone. Make sure you pay careful attention to your phone, the buttons and anywhere you get stuck with dust and pocket lint.

Also, make sure to remove any case that is on your phone or laptop, clean it below, put it on and clean it outside. Following the CDC instructions for other high-touch surfaces in the house, disinfecting the devices once a day should not be harmed.

How to clean your laptop displays from your computer is not always made of glass (matt displays are of plastic) to prevent the use of a wipe disinfectant, if only. The panel should be washed with the soft towel (70 percent) and isopropyl alcohol solution. Make sure you wipe down the keyboard, trackpad, outside and on your laptop wrists.

Most computers on the desktop are still in great need of cleaning. A disinfecting cloth or isopropyl alcohol solution and a warm towel are the perfect way to do this.

Again, even in the event of disinfecting wipes on the display, stick to isopropyl alcohol. But otherwise, just wipe the mouse down (top, hand, and bottom), the keys on your keyboard, the keyboard outside and any mousepad.

For any other electronic product, when the exterior is mostly plastic (gaming mice, gamepads, television remotes) it is necessary to provide them with a disinfectant cleaning or isopropyl alcohol solution once in a while.

Essential rules:

Stay at home, with the exception of important food visits, etc.

Wear a fabric face mask in public. (Here's how to make a mask and the rules surrounding it.) Keep in public at least 6 meters away from other people.

Once, always wash your hands for at least 20 seconds (or using a hand sanitizer if you cannot scrub).

Cough or sneeze into your elbow's tissue. Do not touch your face.

Cloth Face Mask Investing

CDC has reversed their advice on face masks. It now advises that everybody wear a face mask. We do and do not have detailed instructions on masks in our CDC-approved facial mask guide.

Masks are an added precaution to stay home, wash your hands, distance from society and the other directions that you should follow. It is unlikely that a cloth mask can keep you from having the virus, but it can help protect others if you get the disease.

Some people with the disease have mild or no symptoms — especially young people. You might have it and you do not know. We recognize that the current virus is transmitted through human touch or respiratory droplets. Simply talking to others will bring droplets.

Do not put a mask on children under 2 or buy a N95 mask or a professional mask to assist medical workers. A serious shortage of masks still exists in the United States, and N95 masks should be for physicians.

This is why the CDC suggests, again, this you make your own mask at home. Please follow our instructions for making a DIY face mask correctly.

To clean and disinfect your home virus, the first thing you may want to remember is that cleaning and disinfecting are two things that are very different. The CDC suggests that we do both, even if nobody is sick in your house.

Cleaning is the surface degradation of pollutants.

Disinfecting is for pathogens destruction.

Use this every day whether something or someone has entered or left your house.

The transmission from person to individual is much riskier than the transmission through the air, but the CDC suggests that at least once a day we clean and disinfect high-touch surfaces at home so that we can be safe if we have any contact with the outside world if a person leaves or returns, or products arriving.

CHAPTER 7: Disinfectant Spray Tips & Recipes

This all-purpose disinfectant floor cleaner can be used on hardwood, laminate, carpet, linoleum and tile floors. You may want to use marble and granite sparingly.

Floor Cleaning Disinfectant

Ingredients
2 Cups of Warm Water
1/2 Cup of White Vinegar
1/4 Cup of rubber
3 Drops Dish soap
5-10 Drops of option essential oil such as tea trees of oil

Instructions
Mix all the ingredients in a wide tub. Place the natural disinfectant in a plastic spray bottle until combined. Shake well before using and spray on any cleaning surface. Clean the solution with a mop. Remark: Do not use Castile soap or other oil-based soap.

Homemade Disinfectant For Countertops

The kitchen may easily transform to the messiest space in the home. If you want to remain safe and prevent getting ill, keeping counters clear of germs and bacteria is essential. This is one of our favorite bricolage recipes, because only two ingredients are needed: water and hydrogen peroxide.
Combine water and hydrogen peroxide equal parts and pour in a spray bottle. Spray on the countertops of your kitchen as needed and clean it off using a sponge. It disinfectant can also be used on the tiles of the bathroom or on some other rough surface prone to germs.
This natural disinfecting spray uses the antifungal and antibacterial strengths of essential oils, like tea tree oil, to kill germs and prevent bacteria from overcoming them. This is suitable for yoga mats, fitness equipment and every other bacterial board.

DIY Natural Disinfectant

Ingredients
Sprinkle 3/2 Cup of Water Hazel
10 Drops Tea Tree Essential Oil
5 Drops Eucalyptus Essential Oil
Instructions
Fill a sprinkler bottle with all the ingredients and secure the deck. Shake well to ensure the balance of all components. Spray on every disinfecting surface and then wipe clean. Until using, shake the solution as the oil separates.

Homemade Disinfectant Wipes

Ingredients
1 Poker Filtered Water
1 Poker White Distilled Vinegar
1/2 Poker Alcohol
15 Pokers Lemon Oil
8 Pokers Lavender Essential Oil
4 Pokers Bergamot Essential Oil
1 Mason Jar
15-20 Pieces of Pre-Cut Cloth or Small Washcloths

Instructions
Combine all components in a wide-mouth glass masonry jar or similar. To combine, cover lid and swirl. Press cloths or washcloths in the jar till all fabric is soaked with liquid disinfectant. Replace cover in dark space and stack it.
As required, take a towel and squeeze out the excess fluid to use the disinfectant wipes. Use on any surface of glass, stainless steel, tile, linoleum or porcelain.
This natural spray disinfectant recipes and cleaning tips can clean your house. The gentle natural ingredients are perfect to clean without worries without breaking the bank. Such recipes will only free your home from toxic

chemicals, but you can also take action to become environmentally friendly. Learn how to spray homemade disinfectants with natural ingredients such as vinegar, alcohol paste, vodka, water and essential oils. Such homemade cleaners will envy all your neighbors to your house.

Deep Cleaning Spray

Here is a perfect recipe for a safe and efficient deep cleaning spray. It smells fresh and healthy, and in a rush it kills these germs!

Please note: This DIY was developed long before Virus and has not been evaluated for virus disinfection effectiveness. Please note: For disinfecting advice, please review the CDC.

Gather the ingredients:

1 1/4 cup of water

1/4 cup of white vinegar

1/4 cup (60% plus alcohol content) vodka or alkaline (excellent germ-murdering properties – rusting alcohol can be replaced, but its're more healing),

15 drops of essential oil – peppermint + lemon or lavender + lemon are great in this glass spray bottle.

Instruction

When you mix your water, shake it and sprinkle it off.

I like to thoroughly spray all surfaces, allow them to sit down for about 10 minutes (to avoid germs) and clean them with a microfiber.

It is important to prevent cross contamination in the bathroom, so I wipe separate cloths – mirror, sink, bath / dusche, toilet in that order. Go to my 15-minute bathroom cleaning plan for this chapter.

The same guidelines apply for cross-contamination when using this spray in the kitchen – use different cloths for separate areas. This recipe does not need rinsing.

CONCLUSION

In order to disinfect a surface, the most important factor, by far, is what is called 'dwell time': the amount of time the disinfectant needs to stay on its surface to kill pathogens in general and specifically the virus that causes VIRUS.

Prepacked wipes or paper towels that you used to clean surfaces are easier to dispose of. Retractable cloths and mops 'can always be exchanged for a new one after a cleaning process and then laundered.'

They are used for no more than three rooms in medical facilities until they are cleaned. With a shortage of paper towels, reusable cloths might also be the way to go home — we hope you can always find a washing detergent.

CDC advises in particular the use of "minimum 70 percent alcohol" as a disinfection tool for the any virus, which is the strength of most drugstores with rubbing alcohol, both in liquid form and on pre moistened cleanings. In the guide to medical equipment disinfection, the CDC states that alcohol is effective in one minute on viruses.

The CDC does not prescribe hydrogen peroxide to surface removal of the virus, but it is considered an almost universal disinfectant and a recent study has found that the virus "can be efficiently inactivated by surface disinfection" in one minute by 0.5% hydrogen peroxide.

Alcohol and hydrogen peroxide rubbing are healthy on virtually any hard area and on most fabrics, although it is worth checking them in a dressed environment or in a paddock to ensure that they do not harm the taint. The hydrogen peroxide is separated into water and oxygen gas and evaporates alcohol coating, so that no film or residue is left behind.

Now, a note on the use of whiskey, a disinfectant alleged to be. "alcohol" applies in the health world to rubbing alcohol and ethanol, the latter being the form some people drink. The CDC only finds ethanol efficient at rates of 70% or more.

Many studies suggest that 60% is enough. In any case, vodka is not a disinfectant: it is only 40% ethanol (80 evidence). Extremely over proof liquor can be used in principle.

The Ever clear 151 (75.5% ethanol/151 evidence), the Ever clear Grain Alcohol (90% ethanol/190 evidence) and the Spiritus Rektyfikowany (96% ethanol/192 evidence; ask only for "Spiritus") can be found at your nearest spirits shop. They are highly inflammable, so be careful, especially on the stove.